Southern FOSSIL discoveries • vol. 1

Ice Age Giants of the South

Judy Cutchins and Ginny Johnston

🍍 Pineapple Press, Inc. • Sarasota, Florida

Acknowledgments

The authors wish to thank the following individuals for their expertise in developing our book: Richard Hulbert, Ph.D., Associate Professor of Geology and Museum Curator, Georgia Southern University, Statesboro, Georgia; S. David Webb, Ph.D., Curator of Vertebrate Paleontology, Florida Museum of Natural History, Gainesville, Florida; C. Andrew Hemmings, graduate research assistant, University of Florida; Patty Crews, Geologist, Jacksonville, Florida; and Ed Hooks, Ph.D., Paleontologist and Collections Manager, Alabama Museum of Natural History, Tuscaloosa, Alabama.

We also gratefully acknowledge a number of individuals for their assistance in research and in photograph acquisition: Erika H. Simons, Florida Museum of Natural History, Gainesville, Florida; Cynthia Ryals, Daytona Museum of Arts and Sciences, Daytona, Florida; Fred Grady, National Museum of Natural History, Washington, D.C.; Eric Taylor, Florida Paleontological Society, Lake City, Florida; Lucky Lowe, Brunswick, Georgia; Dr. Cliff Jeremiah, Jacksonville, Florida; Lawrence A. Wilson, Ph.D., Fernbank Science Center, Atlanta, Georgia; and Geb Bennett, Dallas Museum of Natural History, Dallas, Texas.

Copyright © 2000 by Judy Cutchins and Ginny Johnston

All rights reserved. No part of this book may be reproduced in any form or by any means, electronic or mechanical, including photocopying, recording, or by any information storage and retrieval system, without permission in writing from the publisher.

Inquiries should be addressed to:

Pineapple Press, Inc.
P.O. Box 3899
Sarasota, Florida 34230
www.pineapplepress.com.

Library of Congress Cataloging-in-Publication Data

Cutchins, Judy.
    Ice age giants of the South / Judy Cutchins and Ginny Johnston.
      p.   cm. — (Southern fossil discoveries)
    Includes index.
    Summary: Chronicles recent archaeological discoveries of fossils in the Southern States.
    ISBN 1-56164-195-2
    1. Prehistoric animals—Juvenile literature. 2. Vertebrates, Fossil—Juvenile literature.
3. Archaeology—Southern States—Juvenile literature. [1. Prehistoric animals. 2. Fossils. 3. Paleontology.]
I. Johnston, Ginny. II. Title. III. Series.

QE842.C88 2000
566—dc21   99-087670

First Edition
10 9 8 7 6 5 4 3 2 1

Design by Carol Tornatore
Printed in China

Contents

1. Fossils of Giant Mammals   4
2. Great Glaciers   8
3. Life along a Pleistocene River   12
4. Land Bridges Between Continents   20
5. Caves and Sinkholes   22
6. Discoveries in Florida Sinkholes   25
7. Miles and Miles of Grasslands   32
8. Stories Told by Teeth   38
9. What Happened to the Giants of the Ice Age?   44

    Glossary   46

    Scientific Names   47

    Index   48

One

Fossils of Giant Mammals

During the long cool periods that gave the Ice Age its name, the earth was not frozen solid. Worldwide, average temperatures dropped only a few degrees, but it was enough to add ice to the glaciers over time. For thousands of years, the glaciers grew, but they never covered the earth. In regions south of these tremendous ice sheets, there was a variety of habitats for plants and animals. Amazingly, some habitats were in tropical climates. The South, from Texas to South Carolina, was a very warm region throughout the Ice Age.

Scientists know saber-toothed cats, mammoths, mastodons, and many more Ice Age animals lived in the South because their fossils have been found. When animals die, their softer parts (skin, flesh, muscles, organs) decay rapidly. Harder teeth and bones take longer to decay, and there is a better chance that they may become fossilized.

Why So Big?

The huge sizes of fossil bones prove that many prehistoric animals were giants. Some scientists believe large body size is an adaptation to cooler, drier climates. Others suggest that animals gradually become larger when food is plentiful.

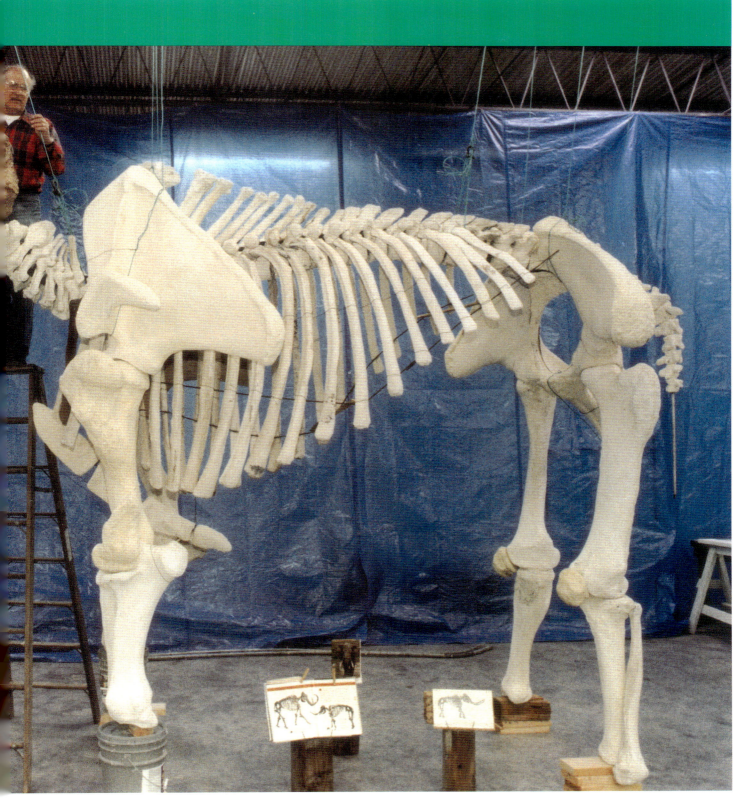

The largest mastodon ever discovered in North America was found in northern Florida's Aucilla River in 1968. Nicknamed "Priscilla," the skeleton is 11 feet tall. (Don Burk, *Florida Times-Union*, Jacksonville, FL)

A researcher from the University of Florida uncovers a leg bone of an extinct giant ground sloth. (Florida Museum of Natural History, Gainesville, FL)

Divers find large fossils like this mastodon vertebra (backbone) on the bottom of southern rivers. (Gene Middlebrooks)

Fossil bones and teeth are not the only clues to the past. Preserved dung (waste material), stomach contents, wood, pollen, and seeds have also been found. Paleontologists use these clues to determine which plants and animals lived in the South during the Ice Age and what their habitats were like.

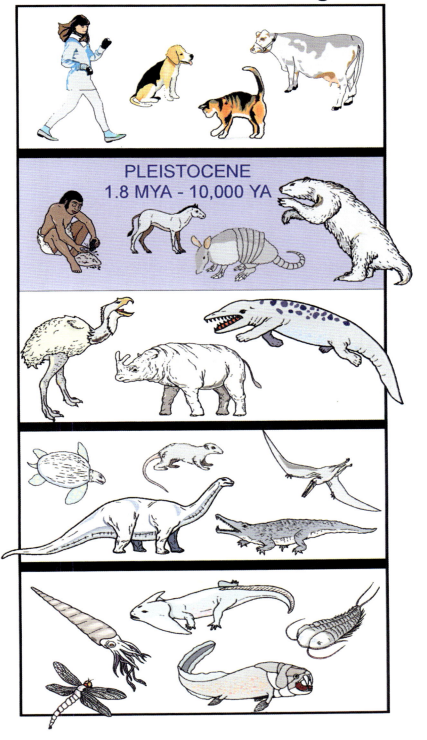

two

Great Glaciers

Most of the Ice Age was during the Pleistocene period. It began almost two million years ago and ended about ten thousand years ago. The Pleistocene started with a long, worldwide cooling trend called a glacial period. With cooler temperatures, glaciers grew and covered the northern regions of Asia, Europe, and North America. The water in the glaciers came from the oceans. As glaciers grew, sea levels dropped.

Scientists believe that glacial periods occurred dozens of times throughout the Pleistocene. Between the long glacial periods, warming trends, called interglacial periods, occurred that may also have lasted thousands of years. During interglacial periods, glaciers melt and the melt water flows into rivers that run to the sea. Sea levels rise. Today, the earth is in an interglacial period.

The most recent glacial period began about 70,000 years ago. By 20,000 years ago, glaciers had advanced over land farther than ever before and sea levels were at an all-time low. There is a strong connection between sea levels and climate. Glacial and interglacial periods affect land and all living things worldwide.

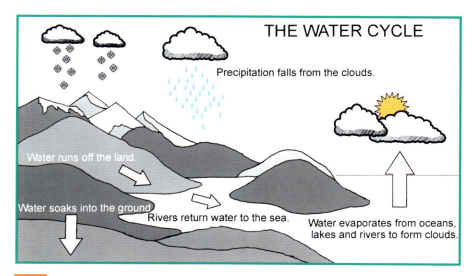

Water evaporates from oceans and later falls as precipitation, such as rain or snow. Over colder regions, if snow does not melt, it can build up as glacial ice for thousands, even millions, of years. (Judy Cutchins)

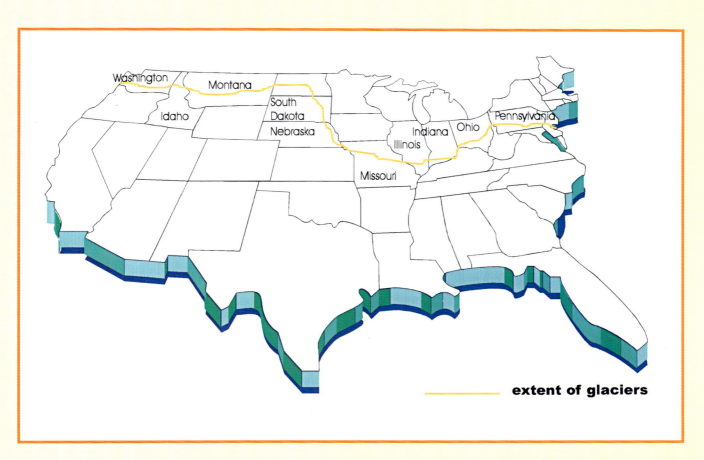

During the coolest glacial period, ice sheets covered much of North America.
(Judy Cutchins)

three

Life along a Pleistocene River

If you could travel back in time thousands of years to an area along a slow-moving river in the South, you might see ground sloths 15 feet tall reaching for leaves to eat. Tapirs, capybaras, and giant beavers would be swimming and looking for food along the riverbank. You might see a huge tortoise, a strange glyptodont the size of a car, or a six-foot-long armadillo in the underbrush. Sound impossible? Scientists know that these animals lived in the South during the Ice Age because southern river bottoms, marshes, and limestone layers are treasure chests of Ice Age fossils.

A giant sloth thigh bone (femur) is hauled from the tea-colored water of Georgia's Frederica River. (James N. Skeen)

What Is a Fossil's Age?

Modern scientists have many methods to help them find out the age of a fossil. In one method, they measure the very small amount of radioactive carbon in a fossil. Older fossils have less "radiocarbon" than younger ones. This method works only for fossils younger than 50,000 years old, the most recent part of the Pleistocene. Fossils older than this do not have enough radiocarbon to measure. These fossils must be dated using other methods.

Giant Sloth

In 1990, amateur treasure hunters were scuba diving in the Frederica River near Brunswick, Georgia. They were searching the muddy bottom for old bottles, pottery, and other treasures when they discovered two fossil bones of an extinct giant ground sloth. The bones had been buried in the mud along the riverbank for more than 30,000 years before the river eroded the bank and washed them out.

The divers searched one area of the river bottom in their quest for more of the extinct sloth's skeleton. Their job was difficult because the water is the color of dark tea, stained by decaying marsh plants. Coastal rivers like the Frederica are known as "blackwater" rivers. It is impossible to see even a few feet below the surface. These divers were very lucky and found most of the sloth's bones. Scientists determined this giant sloth would have weighed about 5,000 pounds and stood more than 15 feet tall—truly an Ice Age giant.

Giant ground sloths were herbivores (plant-eaters) that lived in warm forest habitats near water. Propped on its thick tail, a giant sloth used its huge claws and powerful arms to bend or break branches. A sloth could wrap its long tongue around leaves and pull them into its mouth much like a giraffe does today.

Big Bones, Heavy Bodies

The large size of an animal's leg bone gives paleontologists clues about how heavy the animal was. The giant ground sloth was extremely heavy and slow moving. It had few enemies because of its huge size, thick skin, and long claws.

The three-foot-long femur is whole and is covered by muddy river-bottom sediment. (James N. Skeen)

Giant sloth fossils have been found in South America, Central America, and southern North America. This skeleton is on display at the Daytona Museum of Arts and Sciences in Daytona, Florida. (Daytona Museum of Arts and Sciences, Daytona, FL)

The largest sloth claw ever discovered (shown here) is in the collection of the Florida Museum of Natural History in Gainesville, Florida. (Judy Cutchins)

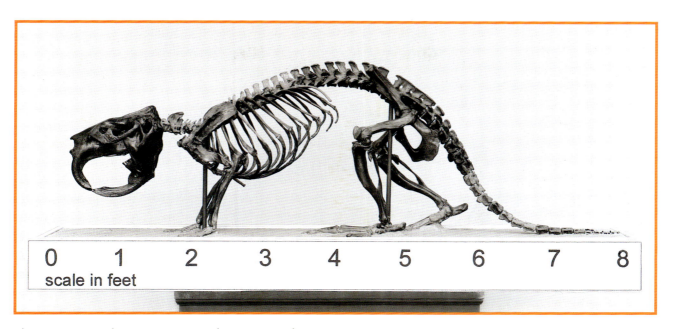

The extinct giant beaver was more than twice as long as a modern beaver. It is thought that these animals were not able to gnaw trees because of their blunt teeth. (Field Museum, Chicago, IL [GEO 79897])

Giant Beaver

Rodents, such as rats, bats, and squirrels, were common in almost every Pleistocene habitat. One of the biggest rodents ever to live was the giant beaver. It was eight feet long from its nose to the tip of its tail. The giant beaver looked like a huge version of its modern relative and was probably an excellent swimmer. But its teeth were different from those of modern beavers. They were more rounded and blunt, possibly used for uprooting water plants instead of cutting down trees. There is no evidence that the extinct giant beavers built dams.

Modern beavers use sharp teeth to gnaw down trees and strip off the bark. (Judy Cutchins)

Capybara

The largest rodents alive today are pig-sized capybaras. They earned their nickname, "water hogs," because they are excellent swimmers. During the Pleistocene, thousands of capybaras lived along the rivers of the southern United States and fed on plants at the water's edge.

Although capybaras have not lived in North America for almost 9,000 years, they are not extinct. They live in tropical South and Central America. (Lawrence A. Wilson)

Whose Bone Is It Anyway?

Entire fossil skeletons are rarely found in the South. More often, the discovery is a single bone or tooth. Experts can easily identify what part of a skeleton a fossil is (rib, leg, skull, etc.), but determining which animal it came from is harder. If the scientists can match a fossil to one in a complete skeleton found somewhere else, they can tell what the animal was.

Tapir

From fossil clues, it is clear that tapirs were common in many regions around the world during the Pleistocene. In North America, their fossils have been found not only in the South, but also in western, mid-western, and north Atlantic states. Prehistoric tapirs were very similar to living tapirs. These cow-sized mammals lived along riverbanks, where they could swim, wallow in the mud, and hide in dense vegetation.

Tapirs are now found only in South America, Central America, and Southeast Asia. A tapir's flexible snout is used to sniff out leaves, buds, and tender shoots. (Lawrence A. Wilson)

Giant Armadillo

Giant armadillos lived during the Ice Age and grew as big as bears. They lived in warm habitats of both North and South America. Paleontologists have studied fossil jaws and teeth and believe the extinct giant armadillo's diet was different from that of its modern relatives. The Pleistocene giant ate grass, while the rare South American giant armadillo that lives today feeds mainly on ants and termites.

Armadillos in North America today are about two feet long and weigh just a few pounds. The Ice Age giant armadillo probably weighed several hundred pounds. (Judy Cutchins)

This jaw of an extinct giant armadillo was found in a Florida limestone quarry by an amateur fossil hunter. Scientists measured the length of the fossil jaw and compared it to the jaw size of a modern armadillo. Then they estimated how long the body might be and decided the giant armadillo was at least six feet long. (Judy Cutchins)

Glyptodont

Nothing like the car-sized glyptodont lives today. And no complete glyptodont skeletons have been discovered in the southern United States. Some nearly complete skeletons have been assembled in other parts of North America.

Paleontologists know that glyptodonts lived along the southern coast from Florida to Texas because their bony scutes have been found in these states. This giant mammal of the Pleistocene looked like a huge turtle, but it was more closely related to the armadillo. Each glyptodont had about 2,000 scutes that made up its armor. Short, thick leg bones supported hundreds of pounds of weight. The animal could plow into thorny underbrush for protection from predators. Paleontologists believe glyptodonts used their feet to dig for grubs and insects.

The Present Unlocks the Past

Studying the behaviors of living animals, such as tapirs, tortoises, and capybaras, provides clues about their extinct ancestors. The life of a glyptodont, however, is more of a mystery because no relatives of the glyptodont live today.

This glyptodont is on exhibit at the Field Museum in Chicago, Illinois. (John Weinstein, Field Museum, Chicago, IL [GEO 85599-4])

A single scute, or bony plate, of an armor-covered glyptodont is easy for fossil hunters to recognize because of its unusual appearance. Many scutes have been found in the South. (Judy Cutchins)

Tortoise

Tortoises are land turtles. Some of the biggest tortoises today live on the tropical Galapagos and Aldabra Islands. A giant tortoise may weigh 500 pounds and reach more than five feet in length. Without teeth, the tortoise's beak acts like garden clippers to snip tough grasses, cactus fruit, and leafy twigs. In North America, there are no longer any tropical habitats where giant tortoises survive. Only their fossil shells remain to tell paleontologists these huge reptiles once lived here.

Top: Although a tortoise shell looks like one solid cover, it is actually made of many flat pieces. Scientists at the Florida Museum of Natural History were able to put the shell of a Pleistocene tortoise back together. (Judy Cutchins)

Bottom: Giant Aldabra tortoises at Zoo Atlanta in Georgia are very much like their Pleistocene relatives. (Judy Cutchins)

Fossil Clues to Past Climates

Sloths, capybaras, and giant tortoises now live only in habitats where temperatures are warm year-round. Finding a giant tortoise fossil is evidence that the location was tropical in the past.

four

Land Bridges Between Continents

Whenever glacial periods occurred and sea levels dropped, more land was exposed around continents. A number of times in the earth's past, dry land connected North America to other continents. These connections are called land bridges. Early in the Ice Age, there was a wide land bridge between North and South America. Over time, it became a grassy plain with scrubby trees and shrubs. Another land bridge connected Asia with North America. Some land bridges were hundreds of miles wide and, like glacial periods, existed for thousands of years.

Plant and animal habitats worldwide were affected by dramatic climate changes. Over generations, grazers and other herbivores thrived in the grasslands. In search of food and new territory, they ventured across the land bridges and eventually into different continents. Naturally, predators followed their prey. Scientists have named this exchange of animals between continents the Great Animal Interchange.

The glyptodont was one of the animals that moved from South America to North America. Giant sloths, armadillos, and many smaller mammals also made their way into North America.

Mastodons came into North America from Asia by way of a land bridge that existed even earlier than the Pleistocene. They lived all across North America and reached South America. Mammoths, lions, saber-toothed cats, wolves, and bison are some other large animals that came here from Europe and Asia. By the late Pleistocene, an enormous variety of animal species thrived in North America.

The Great Animal Interchange went both ways. For example, tapirs, capybaras, and llamas that once lived along riverbanks in North America moved into 21Central and South America. By the end of the Pleistocene, those animals had disappeared from North America altogether. Large predators, such as dire wolves, saber-toothed cats, and lions, also ranged into Central and South America.

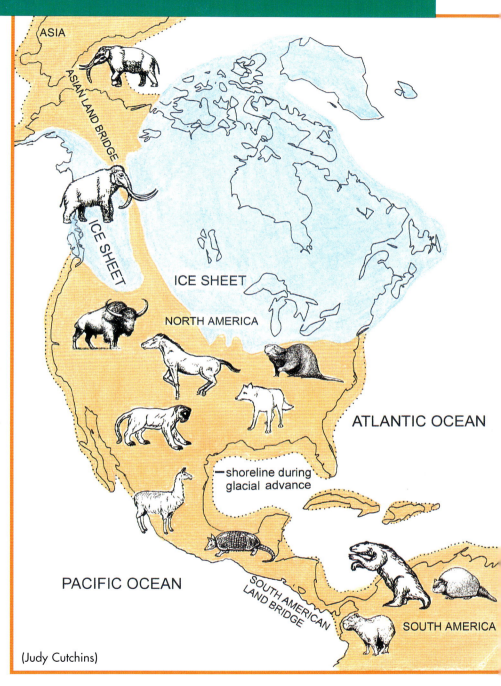

Throughout the Pleistocene, herds of horses thrived on North American grasslands. But, as the Ice Age was coming to an end, climates and habitats began to change drastically. Grasslands in North America were replaced by other types of habitats such as forests or deserts. In some regions of Asia and Africa, however, large areas of grassland still existed. Seeking better grazing lands, herds of horses migrated across the Asian land bridge and onto those continents. By the end of the Pleistocene, there were no horses living in North America. Horses returned only in recent centuries when European explorers brought them back to this continent.

At the end of each glacial period, a warmer interglacial period caused the gradual rise of sea levels. Slowly, land bridges were flooded and some continents, such as Asia and North America, were no longer connected. Land bridges appeared and disappeared dozens of times during the nearly two million years of the Pleistocene.

five
Caves and Sinkholes

Paleontologists exploring a limestone cave in Florida discover the fossilized jawbone of an extinct mammal. (Albert Krause)

Most of the rock that underlies Florida and much of the South is made of limestone. It does not take long for rain and groundwater to erode this soft rock. Erosion forms passageways and caves in the limestone. During the Pleistocene, animals such as dire wolves and saber-toothed cats used caves as dens and hiding places.

When water erodes away enough limestone, a cave becomes an even bigger cavern. If a cavern grows too large, it may no longer be able to support its ceiling of rock and soil. The roof collapses and a sinkhole is formed.

Over time, groundwater levels may rise and fill the sinkhole, turning it into a pond. Soil, sand, leaves, sticks, and other materials wash in and pile up as mucky bottom sediment. Animals fall in or get stuck in the muck when the water is low. If they cannot get out, they die. In time, the mineral-rich mud at the bottom turns bones and teeth into fossils.

Paleontologists have learned that sinkholes can be valuable fossil treasure chests. With careful exploration, scientists can identify what kinds of plants and animals lived in habitats near a sinkhole. Florida and southern Alabama have more sinkholes than any other parts of North America.

How a Sinkhole Is Formed

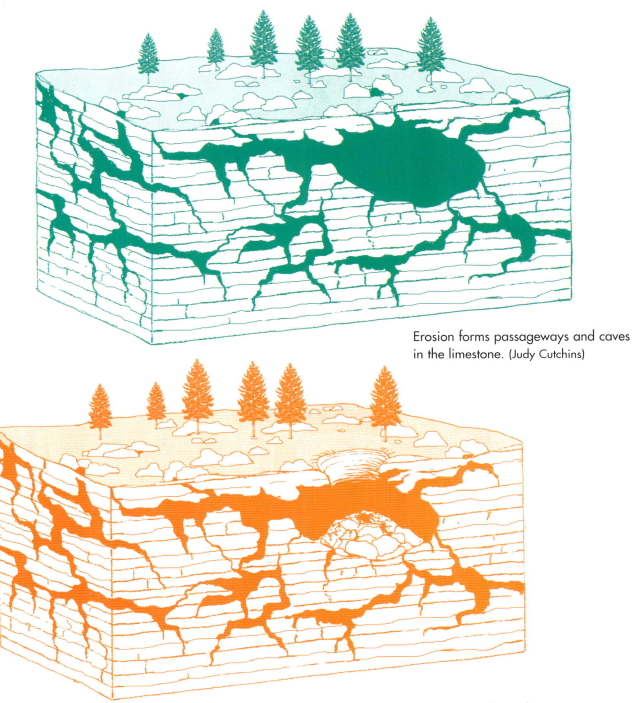

Erosion forms passageways and caves in the limestone. (Judy Cutchins)

A cavern that grows too large cannot support its ceiling of rock and soil; its roof collapses and a sinkhole is formed. (Judy Cutchins)

Digging Back in Time

When scientists dig into layers of sediment like those in the bottom of a sinkhole, they know that the top layers are usually not as old as those below. Digging deeper is like going back in time. Finding fossils of plants and animals in the same layer means those plants and animals probably lived at about the same time.

This fossil hunter uses a safety rope and hard hat to explore a dry sinkhole.
(Florida Museum of Natural History, Gainesville, FL)

Six

Discoveries in Florida Sinkholes

Cutler Hammock

Thousands of Pleistocene fossils were discovered in a small sinkhole a few miles southwest of Miami. The sinkhole and the area nearby are known as Cutler Hammock. Although Cutler Hammock sinkhole is dry now, throughout the Pleistocene it held fresh water from time to time. Fossils of 16 mammal species and many birds, reptiles, and amphibians were discovered at the site. Scientists believe that during the last Ice Age, there was a lush woodland habitat surrounding the sinkhole and a grassland nearby. Animals came to the sinkhole pond to drink.

Evidence of Fresh Water

Amphibians live in and around fresh water. Since amphibian fossils were found in the Cutler Hammock sinkhole, paleontologists know the sinkhole held fresh water some of the time.

About 15,000 years ago, there were many caves in the limestone around Cutler Hammock sinkhole. During years when the sinkhole was not filled with water, it became overgrown with plants. Large carnivores denned and raised young in the hidden caves. Fossils of 42 dire wolves, including pups, were discovered in the sinkhole. Gnawed bones of their prey, including young horses, deer, and mammoths, were also found since carnivores drag prey into their dens. Cutler Hammock sinkhole also had fossils from other large carnivores, such as saber-toothed cats and cave bears.

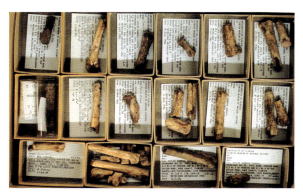

Hundreds of dire wolf fossils found at Cutler Hammock are in the collection of the Florida Museum of Natural History in Gainesville. (Judy Cutchins)

Why So Many Fossils Here?

Finding so many fossils of animals in a sinkhole is a clue that caves were there long before the sinkhole formed. The caves were used by predators and other animals for many, many years.

Dire Wolf

Dire wolves were common in North America during the Pleistocene. A dire wolf had a heavier and more powerful body than a timber wolf, which is the largest wolf species living today.

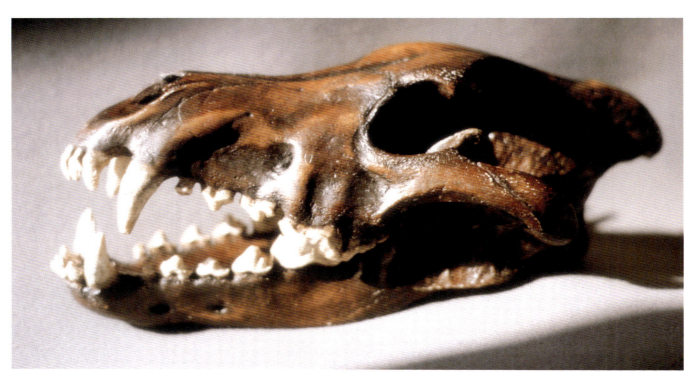

The dire wolf had a larger head and bigger teeth than any past or present member of the wolf family. (Judy Cutchins)

Tooth Marks Tell a Tale

Large and small tooth marks found on bones in the caves mean that dire wolves of all ages were living and feeding there. These clues tell scientists the predators probably lived in packs much like modern wolves.

Saber-toothed Cat

Like dire wolves, saber-toothed cats did not live just in the South. Their fossils have been found in many locations across North America and on other continents. Thousands of saber-tooth fossils have been found in the famous California La Brea tar pits.

The saber-toothed cat was a powerful Ice Age predator. This realistic model is on exhibit at Fernbank Science Center in Atlanta, Georgia. (Judy Cutchins)

A Powerful Cat

The front legs of the saber-toothed cat were large compared to the back legs. This leads scientists to believe that the 600-pound cat probably waited in bushes or tall grass to leap on its prey. It could drag an animal down with its powerful front legs and slash with its saber teeth.

Aucilla River Project

Since the end of the Pleistocene, the earth has been in an interglacial warming trend. Sea levels and fresh groundwater levels in Florida are rising. Today, the Aucilla River flows over dozens of ancient sinkholes in northwest Florida.

For nearly twenty years, researchers from the University of Florida have been diving into the dark waters of the Aucilla and digging into the sinkholes in search of Pleistocene fossils. The divers work with powerful lights and a special vacuum hose. The hose, connected to a pump, sucks sediment from the bottom and shoots it to a platform at the surface. Workers use screens to filter out small fossil bones and teeth. Searching the sediment back in the lab may reveal preserved seeds and even tiny grains of pollen.

Big Clues from Tiny Fossils

No two kinds of plants have pollen grains that are exactly the same size or shape. Scientists study pollen grains under a microscope to identify what kind of plant they came from. Knowing what the plants are provides valuable clues about swamps, grasslands, and forests of prehistoric times.

Divers wear full scuba gear and carry 1000-watt "snooper" lights to see in the 30-foot-deep water of Florida's Aucilla River. (Gene Rowe, Florida Museum of Natural History, Gainesville, FL)

Workers at the surface screen what the vacuum hose shoots up, looking for small fossils. (Florida Museum of Natural History, Gainesville, FL)

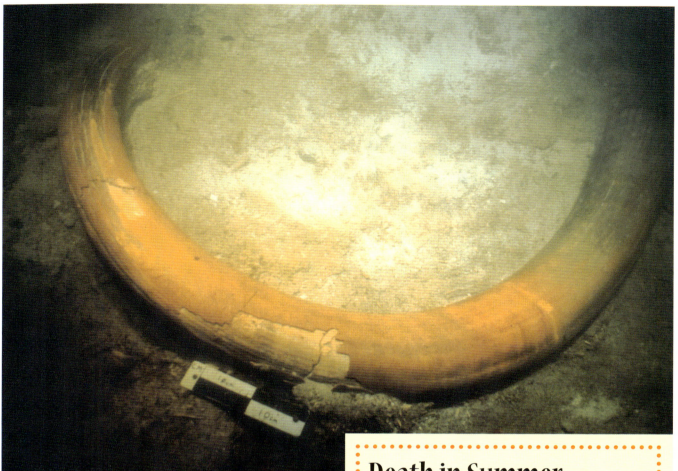

This seven-foot-long mastodon tusk was discovered on the bottom of the Aucilla River. (Florida Museum of Natural History, Gainesville, FL)

Death in Summer

Because grapes and gourds ripen on vines in the summer, finding them where the stomach was in an animal indicates the time of year the animal died. The dry spell that brought so many animals to the sinkhole for water must have occurred during the summer.

In 1995, the Aucilla divers discovered a large number of mastodon fossils piled on top of each other in the muddy bottom sediment. Perhaps during an Ice Age dry spell, the sinkhole was the only watering hole in the area. Mastodons that came to the pool to drink or wallow may have become stuck in deep mud and died there. Yellow, matted-looking straw was found alongside some of the fossils. This proved to be partly digested food preserved in a mastodon's stomach. Chewed twigs, tree bark, and gourd and grape seeds were part of this animal's last meal.

Seven

Miles and Miles of Grasslands

During long glacial periods when sea levels dropped, there was a wide grassland around the Gulf of Mexico from Florida to Mexico. Grazers, such as horses, mammoths, and bison, thrived in these habitats. Huge American lions, wolves, and other predators were also common.

During the Pleistocene, much of the South must have looked like today's African Serengeti Plain. (Lawrence A. Wilson)

American Lion

The greatest predator of its time was the American lion. It is the largest cat ever to live, reaching a body length of over eight feet. Although it is called the "American" lion, fossil evidence of this same species has been found on five continents: North and South America, Europe, Asia, and Africa. No other Pleistocene predator is known to have lived in so many areas of the world.

A horse's front teeth are used for nipping while large jaw teeth grind tough grasses. This Pleistocene horse skull is on exhibit at the Florida Museum of Natural History in Gainesville. (Judy Cutchins)

An American lion skull was found in the Ichetucknee River in northern Florida, but no complete skeleton has been discovered. (Judy Cutchins)

Horse

The earliest horses lived in North America long before the Pleistocene. They were fox-sized animals that lived in forests. These early horses did not have long legs for running across miles of grasslands. But over many generations, horses became larger and well adapted to grassland habitats. They could run for miles across open prairies and had teeth suited to grinding tough grasses.

Bison

Fossils of bison have been found all over the United States, including most of the Southern states. There were several kinds of bison in North America during the Pleistocene. One species had horns that measured five feet across from tip to tip. During the Pleistocene, vast herds of bison, relatives of today's buffalo, roamed grasslands across America.

A Brainy Predator

Measuring the space for the brain inside the American lion's skull shows it had the largest brain of any great cat. Modern cats that live in social groups, called prides, have larger brains than those that live and hunt alone. From this clue, paleontologists believe the extinct American lions may also have lived in prides.

This Columbian mammoth was discovered in Texas and is on display at the Dallas Museum of Natural History, Dallas, Texas. (Geb Bennett, Dallas Museum of Natural History, Dallas, TX)

Fossil researcher Dr. Cliff Jeremiah holds the huge skull of a Pleistocene bison that once lived in the South. (Judy Cutchins)

Mammoth

Only a few elephant species lived during the Pleistocene. The Imperial mammoths were the biggest, standing over 14 feet tall. No fossils of Imperial or woolly mammoths have been discovered in the South, but fossils of the Columbian mammoth have been found. Columbian mammoths lived throughout North America.

eight

Stories Told by Teeth

Teeth are the most common mammal fossils found because most are covered by a rock-hard enamel that fossilizes very well. The amount of enamel on a tooth and the tooth's shape and size provide important clues about what a prehistoric animal ate.

Animals that eat meat are called carnivores. They have pointed teeth with sharp edges to bite and tear meat, as well as bladelike teeth to cut through muscle. Herbivores, which eat only plants, often have scissorlike or clipping teeth in the front of their mouths. They use flat-topped teeth in the back of their jaws for grinding plants. Animals that eat both plants and animals are called omnivores. They need a variety of teeth.

Today's wild horses are grazers like the Pleistocene horses of North America. Grazers eat mainly grass and need vast lands to roam. Grasses have tough fibers inside, and the plants get covered with sand and grit. A horse's grinding teeth need to be large enough to last a lifetime. The front teeth are shaped for snipping grass.

Horse teeth are well adapted for constant grinding because they are covered with wear-resistant enamel. This fossil jaw with teeth is on display at the Alabama Museum of Natural History in Tuscaloosa, Alabama. (Judy Cutchins)

Shapes and sizes of teeth provide clues to what an animal eats. (Judy Cutchins)

What Did the Animals Eat?

To learn more about what prehistoric animals ate, paleontologists study the teeth of animals that live today. They also watch what and how the animals eat. When teeth from a prehistoric animal are similar to those of a living animal, scientists can determine what and how the extinct animal might have eaten.

Left: The 12-inch-long mammoth tooth looks like a shoe with deep treads. The surface, or plate, is made of enamel ridges, which are excellent for grinding. (Judy Cutchins)

Below: The cone-shaped parts, or cusps, of a four-inch-high mastodon tooth worked well for crushing needles of evergreen trees. (Judy Cutchins)

Columbian mammoths were also grazers and had teeth much like those of modern elephants. Scientists study elephants in Asian and African grasslands to get an idea of how mammoths might have lived.

Mammoths lived long lives, and their teeth were replaced as they wore out. A new tooth grew in behind one that was wearing down. The old tooth would gradually move

Different Teeth, Different Diets

Scientists know that with such different tooth shapes and diets, mammoths and mastodons did not live in the same habitat. Mastodons were forest animals while mammoths grazed the grasslands.

This is a giant sloth's lower jaw. Each of the V-shaped, five-inch-long teeth in the lower jaw fits together with a tooth in the upper jaw, making it easy for the sloth to clip twigs and leaves. (Judy Cutchins)

Where Are the Most Leaves?

To meet the needs of its huge body, a giant ground sloth ate a tremendous amount of leafy material each day. This means that the sloth's habitat was most likely a forest.

forward in the mammoth's mouth as the new one replaced it. The new tooth was fully in use by the time the old one fell out.

Browsers are animals that eat leaves and other plant parts that are softer and less gritty than grasses. Mastodons were browsers. They used their trunks to reach for leaves and twigs as well as fruit, nuts, and berries.

Giant ground sloths browsed tree leaves. Their teeth did not need strong enamel-like grazer teeth. In fact, giant sloth teeth had no enamel at all. Species of sloths that lived long before the Pleistocene ate mainly soft grubs and worms. But by the Pleistocene, giant sloths had evolved into browsers. They were feeding on twigs and other plant parts rather than insects and worms. This wore their teeth down faster. Over time, they developed ever-growing teeth. Unlike the mammoth, whose old teeth were replaced with new ones, the giant sloth had teeth that continued to grow as fast as they wore down.

A carnivore's sharp, meat-tearing teeth are called canines. American lions, saber-toothed cats, and dire wolves were some of the largest Pleistocene carnivores. Of these, the saber-toothed cat had the longest canines of any mammal that has ever lived. These nine-inch-long teeth were too long for chewing. Most scientists agree that they must have been used for stabbing or slicing prey.

lion

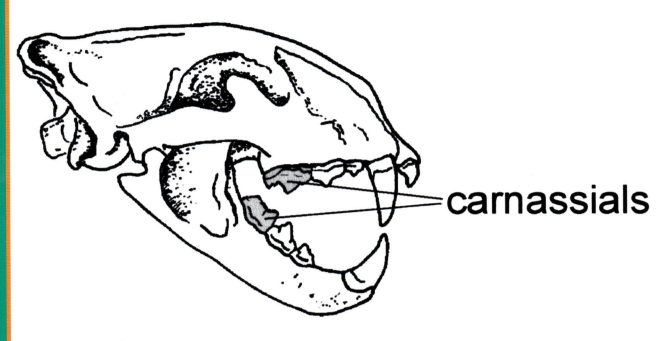

wolf

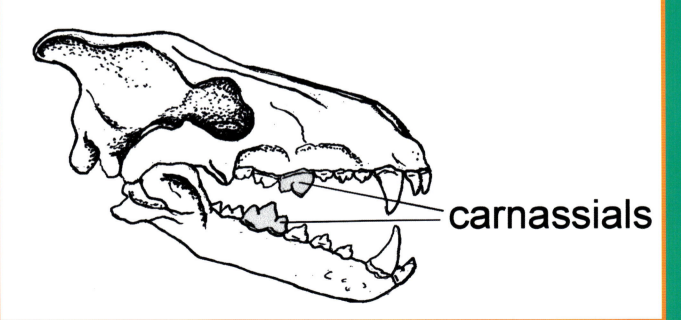

Cats are strictly meat-eaters. They use their carnassial teeth to slice meat from bone, then swallow bites. Wolves have deep jaws and teeth behind their carnassials. This allows them to gnaw bones and eat a wider variety of foods than members of the cat family. (Judy Cutchins)

The saber-toothed cat had the longest canines of any other mammal, living or extinct. (Judy Cutchins)

Slash and Kill

Most of the fossil canine teeth of saber-toothed cats are not chipped or broken. Scientists have used this clue to determine that this predator probably did not bite the bony neck of its prey but instead slashed the soft underbelly.

Behind the canines are teeth called carnassials, which are teeth used for slicing through flesh and muscle. Because cats are meat-eating specialists, their carnassials are well developed.

Members of the dog family, which includes wolves, have molars directly behind the carnassial teeth. These teeth are for grinding and gnawing bone. Unlike the strictly meat-eating cat family, most dogs are omnivores and can eat a wide variety of foods.

Teeth provide important information about the diet, behavior, and habitat of extinct animals. Learning how diets changed throughout the Pleistocene gives scientists clues about how the climate and environment were changing too. This helps them understand when and why certain species became extinct.

More Clues from Teeth

Teeth wear down as an animal ages. Chewing gritty grasses wears teeth even more. The amount of wear on a fossil tooth is a clue to both the animal's age and its diet.

What Happened to the Giants of the Ice Age?

Giant sloths, mammoths, mastodons, dire wolves, and saber-toothed cats were among the dozens of large Ice Age mammals that became extinct about 10,000 years ago. Scientists do not have one simple explanation for their extinction. However, most agree that the worldwide warming trend at the end of the Ice Age played an important role. Melting glaciers, rising sea levels, and changes in climate occurred rapidly. The effects on plant and animal habitats were dramatic. Grasslands that grew across much of North America during the cool, dry times of the Pleistocene were replaced in some areas by woodlands. Broadleaf trees grew where cypress, spruce, and other conifers once thrived. Perhaps many of the giant browsers could not adapt to sudden changes in habitat and diet. Huge herds of grazers were not able to find enough grasslands so their populations grew smaller. Many scientists agree that by the end of the Ice Age, winters were colder and summers were hotter in most of North America. Some regions became deserts. These extreme conditions would have stressed plants and animals. Those that did not adapt became extinct.

About 12,000 years ago, humans began making their way across North America and into regions of the South. Evidence, such as cut marks on fossil bones, spear points, and stone tools, shows that these early people hunted mammoths, mastodons, and other large animals. Some scientists believe that at a time when the giant herbivores were already decreasing in numbers, humans played a role in their extinction.

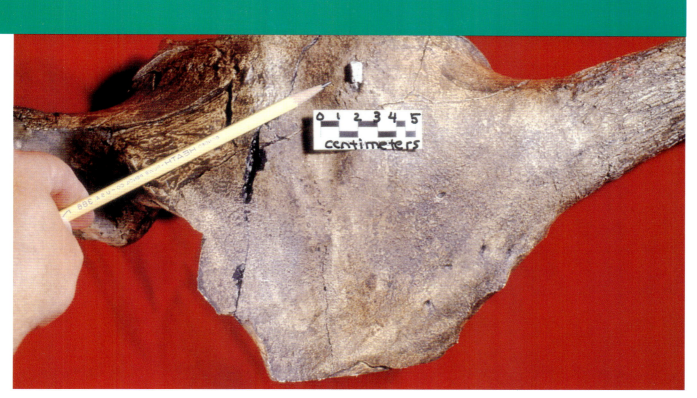

This bison skull, dated at 11,000 years old, has a spear point embedded in it. This rare find in the Aucilla River provides evidence that early humans hunted the giant mammals in Florida. (Florida Museum of Natural History, Gainesville, FL)

Signs of Human Hunters

Scientists have evidence that humans killed giant mammals for food. Some fossil bones have marks on them caused by scraping, such as would occur if early humans scraped meat from the bone. Other bones have char marks where they were burned, perhaps over a cooking fire.

Animal species disappeared at different times on different continents and in different regions of North America. That is because some habitats did not change as rapidly as others. Some of the last large animal species of the Pleistocene survived in habitats of southern North America after they had disappeared from other areas. Opossums, bison, deer, some rodents, birds, reptiles, and amphibians of the Ice Age adapted to new conditions and still live in North America and other parts of the world.

But today almost all the giant land animals of the Pleistocene are extinct. The large number of fossil clues from the southern United States has helped paleontologists learn what this part of the world was like during the Ice Age.

Glossary

Browser—an animal that eats leaves, buds, and soft stems from bushes and trees.

Canines—long, sharp teeth for grabbing and stabbing prey.

Carnassials—teeth behind the canines for slicing meat from bone.

Carnivore—an animal that eats meat.

Climate—general weather conditions in a region.

Fossil—the remains or traces of once-living organisms.

Glacial period—a time when glaciers increase in size and sea levels fall.

Grazer—an animal that eats grass.

Groundwater—underground water that moves through soil and rock layers and can fill sinkholes.

Herbivore—an animal that eats only plant material.

Interglacial period—a time when glaciers decrease in size and sea levels rise.

Limestone—sedimentary rock formed primarily by shells of dead sea creatures.

Omnivore—an animal that eats both plants and animals.

Paleontologist—a scientist who studies fossil evidence to interpret the past.

Pleistocene—the main part of the Ice Age, from 1.8 million years ago to 10,000 years ago.

Sediment—material that settles to the bottom in a body of water.

Sinkhole—a hole in the ground caused when the soil and rock layer over an underground cavern collapses.

Species—a group of related plants or animals with certain traits in common.

Tropical—warm and humid climate year-round.

Scientific Names

Armadillo	*Holmesina septentrionalis*
Beaver	*Castoroides ohioensis*
Bison	*Bison antiquus*
Capybara	*Neochoerus pinckneyi*
Dire wolf	*Canis dirus*
Glyptodont	*Glyptotherium floridanum*
Horse	*Equus occidentalis*
Lion	*Panthera atrox*
Mammoth	*Mammuthus columbi*
Mastodon	*Mammut americanum*
Saber-toothed cat	*Smilodon fatalis*
Sloth	*Eremotherium laurillardi*
Tapir	*Tapirus veroensis*
Tortoise	*Hesperotestudo crassiscutata*

Index

Illustrations are noted by bold page numbers.

American lion, 20, 21, 32, 41
    comparison with modern lion, 36
    description of, **34**, 36
    skull of, **36**
    teeth of, 41
armadillo, extinct giant, **11**, 12, 20
    comparison with modern armadillo, 17, **17**
    description of, 17
    jaw of, **17**
beaver, giant, **10**, 12
    comparison with modern beaver, 15, **15**
    description of, 15
    skeleton of, **15**
    teeth of, 15, **15**
bison, 20, 32
    description of, **34**, 36
    skull of, **37**, **45**
capybara, **11**, 12, 19, 20
    description of, 16, **16**
cave, 22–23, **22**, **23**, 25, 28
climate changes, 4, 8, 19–21, 44, 45
dire wolf, 21, 22, 25, **26**, **27**, 29, 44
    comparison with modern wolf, 28
    description of, 28
    fossils of, 25, **25**, 28
    skull of, **28**
    teeth of, **28**, 41, 43
extinction, Ice Age, 44, 45
fossils
    age of, 12, 24 (*see also* radiocarbon dating)
    recovery of, 6, 13, 30, **30** (*see also* listings for individual animals)
giant ground sloth (*see* sloth, giant ground)
glacial period, 8, 9, 20, 21
glacier, 4, 8, 44
    extent of coverage, **9**
glyptodont, **11**, 12, 20
    description of, 18
    skeleton of, 18, **18**
grasslands, 21, 25, 30, 32, **32–35**, 36, 40, 44

Great Animal Interchange, 20, 21
horse, 21, 25, 32, **34**
    description of, 36
    skull of, **36**
    teeth of, 36, 38, **39**
humans, evidence of, 44, 45, **45**
interglacial period, 8, 21, 30
land bridge, 20, 21, **21**
lion, 42, **42** (*see also* American lion)
mammoth, 4, 20, 25, **26**, 32, 44
    description of, **35**, 37, 40, 41
    skeleton of, **37**
    teeth of, 40, **40**, 41
mastodon, 4, 20, 40, 41, 44
    description of, 5, 31
    fossils of, **6**
    skeleton of, **4–5**
    teeth of, 40, **40**
    tusk of, **31**
radiocarbon dating, 12
saber-toothed cat, 4, 20–22, 25, 44
    description of, 29, **29**
    skull of, 43, **43**
    teeth of, 41, 43, **43**
sea level, 8, 21, 30, 32, 44
sinkhole, 22, **22**, 23, **23**, **24**, 25, 28, 30, 31
skeleton (*see listings for individual animals*)
sloth, giant ground, **10**, 19, 20, 44
    description of, 12–14,
    fossils of, 6, **6**, **12**, **13**, 14, **14**
    skeleton of, 14, **14**
    teeth of, 41, **41**
tapir, **11**, 12, 20
    description of, 16, **16**
timeline, **7**
tortoise, extinct giant, **10**, 12
    comparison with modern tortoise, 19, **19**
    description of, 19
    shell of, **19**
water cycle, 8, **8**
wolf, 20, 28, 32, 42, **42**, 43 (*see also* dire wolf)